Customer Communications

The New Marketing Discipline

John R. Klug, CEO
Thad D. Peterson, President

CCG

Customer Communications Group, Inc.
12600 W. Cedar Drive
Denver, CO 80228
303-986-3000

©1993
Customer Communications Group, Inc.

Published by:
Customer Communications Group, Inc.
12600 West Cedar Drive
Denver, Colorado 80228

Copyright © 1993 by Customer Communications Group, Inc.

All rights reserved. No part of this book may be reproduced or transmitted in any form or by any means, electronic or mechanical, including photocopying, recording, or by any information storage and retrieval system, without permission from the publisher.

Printed in the United States of America

ISBN 0-9639491-2-8

First printing: November 1993

Dedicated to your most important asset... your customers!

"If an institution becomes great, it is usually by the consent of the people it serves."

– A.P. Giannini
Founder, Bank of America

Contents

INTRODUCTION 1

CHAPTER ONE
Why Bother? 3

CHAPTER TWO
Guess Who's Playing Music at
the American Marketing Funeral 11

CHAPTER THREE
The Coming Customer
Communications Revolution 17

CHAPTER FOUR
What's Different
About a Customer? 23

CHAPTER FIVE
What's a Customer Worth? 27

CHAPTER SIX
The Brave New World of
Customer Communications 31

CHAPTER SEVEN
What's Going On ... and Why? 39

CHAPTER EIGHT
The Right Tool for the Job —
Do You Need Advertising,
or Customer Communications? 45

CHAPTER NINE
What's Different About
Customer Communications? 53

CHAPTER TEN
What's *Really* Different About
Customer Communications? 61

CHAPTER ELEVEN
Here's Where We've Been 69

CHAPTER TWELVE
Here's How You Get Started 75

APPENDIX 77

PRINTED ON RECYCLED PAPER

Introduction

The most powerful concepts in all fields of knowledge are, in hindsight, the most simple and obvious.

To that end, we believe that <u>existing customers</u> are every company's most important asset ... and the most neglected.

Yet, your company's marketing has probably focused almost exclusively on acquiring new business ... not on communicating with and retaining the customers you've already got.

Rather than get leftovers, we think that existing customers should be the <u>primary</u> focus of every marketing budget. And, increasingly in the '90s, we think there are powerful economic reasons to do so.

Unlike before, the national income pie is not expanding (or at least not as fast), conspicuous consumption is no longer politically correct, there is less market to share, and competition, especially from foreign sources, is intense for what market share does remain.

The name of the game now is to downsize, divest, hold on to what you've got. Mind the store. Provide value. Take care of existing customers ... build long-term relationships. And, above all, don't let current customers be poached by marauding competitors!

We have found that communicating with and marketing to customers is profoundly different from other types of marketing. For example, implicit in all customer communications should be the assumption that you are speaking with a friend. Sounds simple. Perhaps obvious. But, it's difficult to accomplish successfully!

We've spent nearly two decades working to help companies in many industries communicate with their customers. We think we're skilled at it, and we believe we've learned what does ... and doesn't work.

We appreciate the opportunity to share our experiences with you here.

Thank you for your interest in this exciting marketing discipline. We hope that you'll benefit and profit from the thoughts we present.

John R. Klug
Thad D. Peterson

1

Customer Communications: Why Bother?

- **Communication is the most fundamental of all human (and marketing) activities. Unfortunately, it is also one of the most difficult techniques to use effectively.**

- **The role ... and the potential ... of customer communications in the marketing mix are misunderstood and usually neglected.**

- **Failure to incorporate customer communications into your marketing plans will expose you to risks you've never considered.**

- **Effective customer communications was instrumental to the survival of one of the nation's largest financial institutions — and subsequently to the largest successful recapitalization in history!**

This book is about communications. It's the outgrowth of a very personal experience. And a passionate conviction that John Klug and I share.

Actually, this book is about a very specialized subset of communications that we think is a new and heretofore misunderstood marketing discipline, called "*Customer Communications*."

What Is Communications — A Personal Sojourn

But, before we get into the nitty-gritty of this supposed new discipline, let's tackle something far more fundamental — what is communications?

And, in the marketing context, how is communications different from advertising and promotion? Why is it important? Why should I do it? And, how do I justify the cost? All of these questions we will answer in this book.

You'll Know It When You See It

Let's first look at communications as part of the classic marketing paradigm of **Price, Product, Place** and **Promotion**. Clearly, communications is a subset of

Promotion. It's the way you tell someone about the product or service you have to sell (or maybe reinforce the purchase decision for those who are already customers!). It's related to advertising, PR and all other derivatives of Promotion.

But, communications is different from classical advertising and promotion techniques and is, by far, the most difficult tool in the marketing mix to describe, understand and utilize effectively. It is a little like getting your arms around the definition of pornography — as a frustrated U.S. Supreme Court finally handed down ... "we can't define it ... but we know it when we see it!"

The Most Fundamental of Human (and Marketing!) Activities

Few would disagree that communication is one of the most fundamental and important of all human (and marketing!) activities.

And yet, perhaps because the short-term results of communication are usually hard to quantify in ROI terms, it also can be hard to justify. This explains, in our experience, why the world seems to break down into those who believe in and are committed to communications for its own sake ... and those who are not.

We hope to convince you that communications — and more specifically customer communications — does not need to be justified on blind faith alone. Indeed, it will stand on its own merit ... and rightfully demand a place in your marketing mix. Furthermore, we will show that it is almost always profitable to do so.

In contrast, failure to incorporate a customer communications program into your plans actually reduces your most profitable sales opportunities and exposes you to risks you never thought of.

A True Story

In 1989 I was hired by Glendale Federal Bank, in California. Glendale was a $20 billion financial institution ... one of the largest in the country. However, like many S&Ls, Glendale fell victim to hard times and, in fact, we were on the government's list of thrifts to be closed down.

One of the first challenges facing our management team was to drastically reduce expenses, and quickly. As Executive Vice President of Marketing, I was told to reduce the marketing budget by 60%, and do it in a way that hopefully minimized the impact on the business.

A Shift in Focus

Well, with a 60% reduction in the marketing budget, traditional advertising and prospect promotion was the first thing to go ... but we needed something (anything) that would keep the business going. We concluded that the most effective and efficient way to hold on to what we had was to shift the focus of all our marketing efforts to our existing customers.

Almost sounds like an oxymoron, doesn't it? "*Marketing to customers*." But it's not, as you will see ....

We quickly built a database marketing system that targeted our best customers, and backed that up with broad-based communications through newsletters. In addition we built a Realtor communication program to help maintain loan volume, and we rolled out the entire effort in six months. That's lightning speed for a bank!

A Communications Infrastructure

Beyond the proactive communication efforts targeted at customers and Realtors, we also built a system to pass all the information we had about the bank to our hundreds of retail branches as quickly as possible.

Anytime something happened, good or bad (and it was mostly bad), a fax went out to every fax machine and branch manager in the company.

That way, every associate had the opportunity to understand the latest news about the company's situation ahead of time, and the front line wasn't caught off guard by a customer's inquiry.

Largest Financial
Recapitalization in History

The result? Despite its brush with death, Glendale Federal is still in business, and in September 1993 completed the largest private recapitalization of a financial institution in U.S. history. Over $450 million of new capital ... not one penny of cost to U.S. taxpayers ... and Glendale is very much moving forward as an aggressive new player in the financial arena.

Throughout our darkest hours at Glendale, we were amazed at how many customers became allies in our cause. Not only did they support us with business and by keeping their funds in the bank ... they also actively lobbied and supported the bank's efforts during difficult negotiations with the government.

Of course, under the circumstances, we didn't have any way to measure what might have happened <u>without</u> intensive customer communications ... but the consensus is that the situation would have been much worse without it, and, in my opinion, the bank likely would not have survived.

Friends Out of Customers

So why bother? Because sometimes you need the help of your friends ... and customer communications can make friends out of your customers.

I'd rather sell to friends any day. If you think that makes sense, please read on to keep learning more about this exciting new marketing discipline.

Thad D. Peterson

2

Guess Who's Playing Music at the American Marketing Funeral

- ***Traditional marketing and advertising are often like an elixir ... as good feeling, and sometimes as worthless, as snake oil.***

- ***Some of the largest, most powerful, U.S. corporations have been humbled by companies that didn't even exist a decade or so ago.***

- ***No matter what your size today, <u>you</u> can become the dominant force in your market or industry.***

- ***No one can help you more, or put you out of business faster, than your customers.***

If we look over the American business landscape of the last 50 years, we can only marvel. Vast industries have been created, assisted by marketers and their advertising agencies, to help sell a multitude of products and services to a populace all too willing to purchase "the latest and greatest" with their ever-growing disposable income.

The Seeds of Change Affecting Today's Marketing World

About ten years ago, a sea change began. Of course, such cataclysmic changes are rarely obvious at the time. And, even with the rear-view perspective of a decade or more, this one can only be seen in the sketchiest and haziest of terms. Nevertheless, a major change did take place.

First, disposable incomes began to stagnate and even fall in real terms. The result was that competition increased, if only because the overall disposable-income pie was shrinking.

Second, the U.S., which had always been the largest "common market" in the world, began to encounter competition from other major trading blocs, namely, the Europeans and the Japanese. Dollars, which had tended to be continually recycled within the U.S. economy, began to flow overseas.

Third, the insatiable American appetite for petroleum continued unabated, causing even more tens of billions of dollars to flow out of the country.

And finally, vast U.S. deficits that were counted in hundreds of billions were increasingly financed by our overseas allies. In a few short years, we shifted from the largest creditor nation to the largest debtor nation in the world.

All of these dollar shifts, outflows and trading patterns might have been less troublesome if the U.S. export performance had approached the aggressiveness and success of our competitors. In that case, earnings from overseas sales might have largely offset the outflows.

Unfortunately, for reasons which are now well-known, this did not occur.

Something Is Going On

And yet, through it all, traditional marketers continue to play like trumpeters at a New Orleans jazz funeral ... and lead us, happily humming dozens of marketing jingles, many for foreign products, toward inevitable economic Armageddon. "Oh what a feeling!"

How prophetic was the Apple ad during the 1985 Super Bowl, which showed uptight, briefcase-toting corporate executives — seemingly a parody of IBM — blindly following each other in lockstep and marching off the edge of a cliff into the abyss below.

At that time, IBM was one of the largest and most powerful corporations on earth. Apple was a tiny gnat buzzing around the elephant, still being run by renegades who had begun business in a Cupertino garage. And the founder of Dell was hardly old enough to get a driver's license.

Today, less than a decade later, upstarts such as Apple, Dell and Compaq are among the largest sellers of personal computers in the world. In turn, IBM has given up in recent losses nearly one-third of all the money it earned in its entire corporate history!

Would it be acceptable if we scream from the rooftops (and, indeed, from these very pages), *"Something is going on!!!"*

What's going on is that you're being doped with a business narcotic. An elixir as good-feeling (and sometimes as worthless) as the snake oil sold at county fairs earlier this century. You're being led off the edge into the abyss.

The music being played at the American jazz funeral by conventional marketers is stimulating, exciting, soul-stirring ... and potentially economically fatal.

You Can Become the Dominant Force in Your Industry

This booklet is about a revolution. A revolution going on right now that is shuffling the musical chairs in your industry as dramatically as has happened in computers ... and cars ... and machine tools ... even orange juice. (Most comes from Florida ... right? Try Brazil!)

But change brings opportunity, and no matter what your size today ... *you* can overturn the IBM of your market or industry and become the dominant force, no matter what your product or service. Again, it all has to do with two simple but powerful concepts.

One is that you have only one reason to be in business ... that is to profitably satisfy (and, hopefully, *thrill*) your customers. The second is that no one knows more about you and can help you more (or can put you out of business faster) than your present customers.

With that as our mantra, dear reader, read on.

3

The Coming Customer Communications Revolution

- **Every business has only one simple reason for being ... to profitably create and serve customers.**
- **Customers are <u>the</u> asset of your business.**
- **Customers are smart. Don't try to fool them. They know your products and business better than you do.**
- **Look from outside into your business. (From the customer's perspective.) Most of us do just the opposite.**
- **Talk <u>with</u> (not to) your customers.**
- **Communications doesn't follow sales ... it should <u>lead</u> it.**

Let's talk about customers. We'll assume that you know how to *get* them. What we choose to address here is how to relate to customers and *keep* them. In our opinion, that's where the greatest marketing opportunities lie in the 1990s.

Customers Are Your "Raison d'Être" ... and Smart

Everything you'll read herein is driven by two simple premises.

- The first is that every business has only one simple reason for being ... <u>to profitably create and serve customers</u>.

- Second, <u>customers are smart</u>. They will always have a higher propensity to either repeat their purchase (or reject it!) because ... from a customer's perspective, they know more about your product or service than you or any non-customer ever could.

One more thing ... we'd like you to rededicate yourself to the proposition that customers are your most important asset. Not an asset ... *the* asset.

Inside-Out vs. Outside-In

The reason this focus on customers is important is that, if you are like most businesspeople and view your products/service as your principal asset, you continually look from within-to-out.

You'll yell down from your corporate ramparts and talk *to* customers.

And, at best, you'll consider communications as a support function that *follows* the sales effort.

> ■ **Classic example of "inside-out":** The new Chairman, President, and CEO of Ford Motor Company, Alexander J. Trotman, a man with ultimate responsibility for selling more than three million vehicles a year, doesn't own a car.
>
> By his own admission, he has never bought from an American dealer, haggled over price and trade-ins, nor fussed with matters like auto insurance and registration. And he certainly has never confronted the charms of a service department.
>
> "I've never bought a car in America, and don't see why I should. The last vehicle I remember buying was a Japanese motorcycle." *(New York Times, 10/7/93)*

In turn, if you view customers as your principal asset, you'll have an outside-to-within perspective.

You'll walk up the road, eager to talk *with* your customers.

And you'll use a variety of customer-directed communications efforts to *lead* the sales effort.

- **Examples of how some executives attempt to get "outside-in"**: The *NY Times* article also mentions that the late Sam Walton, founder of Wal-Mart and one of the richest people in the country, was famous for dropping into Wal-Mart stores to talk with staff and customers.

   And Ross Perot, during his stormy tenure, loved to needle senior GM executives by donning ragged clothes and going out to visit dealerships to assess service first-hand.

So this "inside-out" versus "outside-in" stuff ... is it subtle? ... Yes. Play on words? ... No. Important? ... absolutely critical!

Here's to getting in touch with your most valuable asset. Long live customers!

4

What's Different About a Customer?

- *You can't fool customers. They're often better judges of your company than you are.*
- *It can cost ten times the marketing dollars to get sales from a prospect, versus a customer.*
- *The more a customer knows ... and trusts you, the less you need to spend on inefficient or inappropriate media to "maintain contact."*
- *Customer communications allows you to increase sales ... while reducing overall marketing costs.*

If customers are so important ... let's be sure we know one when we see one. And, let's also take a look at how you have to market differently to customers. There's more to it than you might think.

Here's What a Customer Is Like

A customer is someone who has bought your product or service.

They have dealt with you, your company and your product enough that you can't fool them.

If your quality is lousy, they already know it. If your customer service and return policy are the pits, a customer knows it. Similarly, if some aspect of your product and the way you do business is superb, they also know that.

In other words, customers have bought enough of what you have to sell and dealt with your company often enough that they probably are more accurate judges of your company than you are.

Customers already have strong feelings about you. Deal with them "where they are," and don't even think about trying to fool them!

And ... Here's the Mindset of a Prospect

A prospect is someone who has not purchased your product or service before and probably knows little about your company.

We could suggest that a prospect has an open mind ... but actually it is more likely that it is closed.

In a society where "caveat emptor" is the norm for most economic activity, the mindset of a prospect coming into any relationship with your product or company is generally one of negativism, or at least skepticism.

That's why it can often take ten times or more marketing dollars to get sales from a prospect than it does to get the same incremental sales from a customer.

The Payoff

The more a customer knows about (and likes) your product or service ... and trusts your company, the less you need to spend on increasingly anachronistic, expensive, inefficient, traditional advertising in order to "maintain contact."

In addition, done properly, marketing to customers almost always gives a better sales return than spending the same money on prospects. Usually by an order of magnitude or more!

Bottom line — money invested specifically to communicate with your customers reduces the need to spend elsewhere. Effective customer communications gives a superior financial return and will almost always reduce your overall marketing costs per unit of sales.

5

What's a Customer Worth?

- *You may be astounded at how much a customer is really worth to you ... and how much you can — and should — spend on an ongoing communications program.*

- *Use "Total Relationship Value" to guide your communications program.*

Recently I was at a seminar with people representing dozens of different businesses. The question was asked by the moderator, "How much is one of your customers worth?"

Note that he didn't ask how much it costs to acquire a customer, but rather, how much is a customer *worth* during the average length of time you'll do business with that customer.

Astounding Numbers

Personally, I was expecting that most people would say their customers were worth several hundred dollars each. I was astounded when the majority of the group said that they felt their customers were worth somewhere between $5,000 and $10,000 apiece. A few said their customers were worth $50,000 each.

Surely, then, we don't need to do academic studies and run elaborate computer models to convince ourselves that we should spend a certain percentage of the value of our customers on effective communications with them.

You Can Afford More Than You Thought

Let's assume that you consider your customers have a total relationship value of, say, only $1,000 each.

And let's further say that you're quite skeptical about this customer communications stuff, and you're only willing to invest 1% per year to keep in touch with your customer base.

Even this $10 per year/customer could still fund an outstanding communications program ... and it's probably much more than you're spending right now.

Depending on the overall size of your customer list, you could do several direct mail letters, outbound telemarketing, inbound 800 number programs, maybe even a proprietary company magazine targeted just at customers.

Do the Numbers

Take the time to think about what your customers are worth to you. How much gross margin will be generated over the expected lifetime of your relationship with a given customer? Use this "Total Relationship Value" to help guide your communications program and to help determine how much you should logically invest to retain your customers.

If you really want to get fancy, you can run a discounted cash flow analysis of that gross margin and compute everything in "present value dollars."

Any way you want to look at it, however, you'll probably be astounded at how much a customer is really worth to you, and how much you can and should allocate to ensure that you maintain an ongoing relationship with your most important corporate asset.

6

The Brave New World of Customer Communications

- **We are no longer "one nation, indivisible..." The melting pot broke. We are thousands of tribes.**
- **People crave to "mix" with their media... not have it thrown at them.**
- **Hollywood and video game designers know more about communication in the '90s than Madison Avenue.**
- **The database becomes the repository of everything you know about your customers. It is <u>the</u> business.**
- **The new world of customer communications is customer-focused, interactive, narrowcast, high bandwidth, multi media, driven by a database, and media-specific to the individual.**

"It's better to send a message than to receive one."
"Sell, don't tell." "Preach, don't teach."
"Catalogs, not dialog..."

This is the world of traditional marketing and communications.
And it's a dead dead world!

R.I.P. Marketing as We've Known It!

Washington Post T.V. critic Tom Shales has observed, "For forty years we were one nation, indivisible, under television." That was the period from 1940 to 1980.

The Melting Pot Melted

Now, however, our melting pot has melted. Columbus Day, and even Thanksgiving, is being attacked by multicultural revisionists.

The founding fathers are being characterized as just another gang of dead European white guys.

And freedom and justice for all, as Debra Goldman pointed out in *AdWeek*, doesn't ring true, "... not if your ancestors came over on slave ships or were herded into reservations or interned in WW II prison camps."

By the 21st century, there will be more women, blacks, Hispanics and Asians in the workforce than white males. We may be one nation under God, but now we're not indivisible anymore. The melting pot truly melted.

The Most Profound Revolution Has Begun

In this new nation of splintered ethnic groups and multicultural "tribes," marketing messages no longer work as well on the broadcast networks. Today's consumers must be increasingly "narrowcasted" in the privacy of their own homes by cable, mail, telephone, or even by direct fax or computer bulletin boards.

"Zappers," "grazers" and "surfers" have taken control of the media channels and are redefining the advertising playing field.

Niche marketing, micro marketing, laser-guided narrowcasting. It's a new ball game. But the most profound revolution of all has just begun.

The advent of a unique new marketing discipline — customer marketing.

Mixing With the Media

The marketplace of the future will be dominated by those companies who recognize that customers are the central focus of every successful business ... and that customers must be addressed differently than prospects.

> *Highly successful companies will cultivate intense, reciprocal, interactive relationships with their customers. And they will devote the resources necessary in order to communicate with their customers ... and fiercely protect them from encroachment by competitors.*

Broadcast messages in traditional media will no longer be effective. You must begin to "narrowcast" your messages. Multimedia will become critical. People crave to "mix" with their media, not just have it thrown at them.

Customers Need Bandwidth

Customers will have to be reached on many levels ... but with high bandwidth, narrowcast media. Don't confuse broadcast, narrowcast and bandwidth.

- Broadcast means you can reach lots of folks all at once, but with only limited ability to target precisely (radio, TV networks like NBC, ABC, etc.).

- Narrowcast means that you have the ability to efficiently reach very specific groups ... right down to a single individual (e.g., fax messages, direct mail, individualized custom newsletters, etc.).

- Bandwidth means you are able to give customers a rich variety of information, often interactively (e.g., a telephone call, fax-on-demand, on-line computer bulletin boards, etc.).

Again, customers need to be narrowcasted as much as possible, but with high bandwidth.

Communications methods we've described above and others such as VHS video mailouts, interactive personal computer software, CDs, video disks, shopping channels, 800 response, even the vast worldwide Internet computer messaging system ... these are examples of interactive, narrowcast multimedia with the capacity for lots of bandwidth.

Ironically, filmmakers and video game designers know more about bandwidth, customer involvement, and how to communicate using the new media of the '90s, than Madison Avenue.

Let's Clear Up Some Jargon

Terms like "narrowcast" and "bandwidth" probably sound like just so much technobabble. The only reason for using such words here is that they are rapidly coming into the marketing lexicon and need to be understood. So let's run through the narrowcast and bandwidth issue one more time to hopefully clarify what we're talking about and drive home its importance.

Consumers don't need *more* information. They are already choking on what's coming at them. So using higher bandwidth media just so you can throw more stuff at customers is not what we're talking about.

The key concept to grasp is that we simultaneously need to evolve to narrowcast/higher bandwidth media so that we can give customers more information *relevant to them as individuals*. To accomplish this enhanced relevance requires narrowcasting but with increased bandwidth.

Look at it this way. Media is like a pipeline. Yes, we are going to use a bigger pipe (more bandwidth) ... but we are also going to use the new capabilities to upgrade the octane (interactivity and personal relevance) and focus better (narrowcast) what we pump through the pipe.

Once more, it's the greater bandwidth that lets us "enrich" the information and make it more relevant to the individual. It is by delivering the information through more narrowcast-type media that we can focus more precisely and efficiently on the appropriate customer.

An Example of Narrowcast/Broadband Communication

In order to break through apathy and traditional advertising clutter to reach a new audience, Coors beer has just begun advertising through PCs using the Prodigy network.

More than two million Prodigy subscribers can now tap into a full menu of updated college football scores and interact with this and other sports information. Of course, the Coors logo and ads for Coors Light are prominently displayed on all screens.

As reported in the *Wall Street Journal*, 9/21/93, Chet Thompson, VP for Prodigy, stated that such advertising will "fundamentally change the advertiser-consumer relationship." How right he is!

The Database Becomes the Business

In order to communicate effectively, it's important to have a precise target. That's why developing, maintaining and using a customer database will become a key business focus of the '90s. The database will tell you who your customers are ... their demographics, lifestyle, past purchases, likes and dislikes.

The database will become the repository of everything known, and to be known, about your customers. As the electronic mirror of your most important asset, the database defines the infrastructure of your customer base. It literally becomes the business.

Consider the database as the detailed map that lets you lay the high bandwidth communications pipelines to your most important asset. You'll need the pipeline in place before you can run a truly effective customer communications program.

Walk the Walk

However, you've got to be careful. Customers may be on the database, but they are not statistics ... they're individuals. For example, one ad for all will no longer work. Every "tribe"... perhaps even every single customer, will eventually receive a different message, a different offer ... and maybe even through a different media. As the Coors example shows, this is not as far away as it sounds.

To communicate effectively with customers, you've got to "walk the walk ... and talk the talk." You must speak out of shared experiences and use the familiar style of friends and confidants. Tone is all-critical. The vernacular is the message. And the media is interactive, involving many technologies that would have seemed like science fiction just a short while ago.

The Brave New World

This is the brave new world of communications. It is customer-focused, interactive, narrowcast, high bandwidth, multimedia, driven by a database, and media specific to the individual.

7

What's Going On...
and Why?

- ***The '80s were "go-go"... the '90s are "hold-hold."***
- ***It used to be 90% to get business/10% to hold. It will become 75% hold/25% get!***

The '80s were the go-go decade. Reaganomics. Rich is better. Get it while you can. The expanding pie theory. Acquire. Promote. Grab for market share. An economic free-for-all.

And, here's how the '80s manifested in virtually every marketing budget.

Marketing Priorities in the '80s

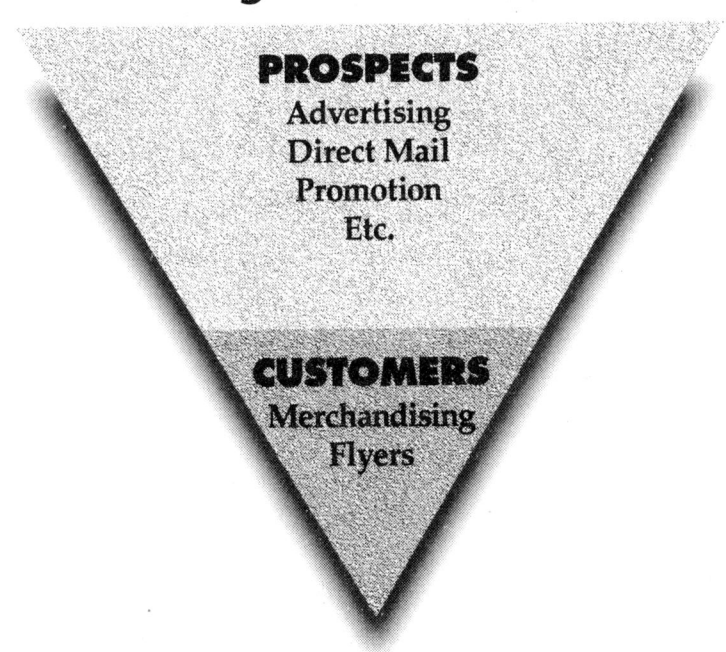

PROSPECTS
Advertising
Direct Mail
Promotion
Etc.

CUSTOMERS
Merchandising
Flyers

Marketing in the '90s

In the '90s, the situation has changed ... the pie is not expanding (or at least not as fast), net disposable household income is declining, conspicuous consumption is not politically correct, there's less market share to share, and competition, especially from foreign sources, is intense for what market share does remain.

Downsize, divest, hold onto what you've got. Mind the store. Provide value. Take care of existing customers ... build long-term relationships. And, above all, don't let customers be poached by marauding competitors.

While it hasn't happened yet in most companies, to be successful in the '90s, here is the way that their generally smaller marketing budgets will need to be recast. (Can you appreciate now what's been happening to traditional advertising agencies, broadcast networks and general magazines like *Time*, etc.?)

Marketing Priorities in the '90s

CUSTOMERS
Database Communications
Proprietary Magazines
Newsletters
Merchandising
VIP Programs
Etc.

PROSPECTS
Advertising
Direct Mail
Promo

The good news is that customer marketing takes a lot less resources for a better return than prospect marketing. So you can communicate with customers and still have money left in your budget to keep the chairman happy with stunning commercials!

In short, the paradigm is shifting. It used to be 90% to get business/10% to keep it. It will eventually shift to perhaps 75% keep/25% get!

8

The Right Tool for the Job... Do You Need Advertising, or Customer Communications?

- **There is a hard way and an easier way to communicate with your customers. You may not have time or the money to take the hard way.**

- **Lawyers and company executives are usually not in touch with the language used by customers.**

- **Effective communications is inversely proportional to the number of approvals required.**

- **Creativeness and effectiveness don't always go together.**

- **The traditional "pyramid" writing style used by most journalists is usually inappropriate for customer communications.**

Some years ago, when we began to focus exclusively on customer communications, we ran into a wall of skepticism from clients ... from our own employees ... and, in fact, even from our own board of directors. No one had ever heard of an agency specializing in customer communications.

"Isn't it just a clever way to make yourself sound different?"

"Couldn't any company call itself a customer communications agency?"

"Isn't all communications the same?"

In other words, "where's the beef?"

Let us illustrate the answer with a story. Among other things, for almost 20 years, our company has been creating custom newsletters which major companies send to their customers. Over the years, we've also watched our clients and others as they sometimes attempt to produce these customer communications pieces themselves. They almost always follow a similar process.

Phase One: "We Can Do It Ourselves"

Quite often, a company begins its customer communications effort with something produced internally. Certainly, this has been greatly helped by the PC desktop publishing technology that has reduced the equipment cost that it takes to put out credible communications, such as an attractive newsletter, from tens of thousands of dollars just a few years ago, to only a few thousand today.

However, because so many product managers, sales executives, marketing directors, lawyers, vice presidents, etc., want to become involved, the time it takes to get out the piece becomes ridiculous, and the copy is reduced to the lowest common denominator. Plus the information is usually product-focused rather than customer-focused.

It's the product manager's, lawyer's and CEO's idea of creative perfection ... but has little relevance to the customer's true needs. Effective communications is inversely proportional to the number of approvals required. In short ... with so many internal constituencies involved ... what comes out is creative pap.

Also, people at the executive level are so far removed from the day to day that they are no longer in touch with the "language" used by their customers. Furthermore, few senior executives are trained communicators. For all these reasons, the entire effort becomes bollixed up in politics and red tape, with inevitable confusion, high costs and failure.

Phase Two: "Send in the Cavalry"

At this point, a consultant is brought in. Typically, a freelance journalist who knows a great deal about writing and communications, but precious little about the industry and customer group involved.

At long last, the newsletter effort proceeds more smoothly, and everyone heaves a sigh of relief. The internal process of getting the newsletter out has been improved ... but not the effectiveness of the communication. Customers are now getting high-quality, irrelevant information instead of mediocre irrelevant information. Somebody eventually wakes up to this fact, and Phase Two comes to an end.

Phase Three: "Bring Up the Artillery"

Finally, someone says, "Let's turn this project over to true professionals at the advertising agency who:

a) know how to communicate, and

b) have worked with us for some time and know our customers and our industry."

Now, of course, the expense has been ratcheted up one more level. The creatives and account types become involved, and a beautiful effort is forthcoming. Both the "process" has been improved, and the copy has become more "relevant" to the customer profile.

Problem is that eventually someone wakes up again and discovers that the effort was ineffectual, if not cost-prohibitive. Why? ... the reason is simple. Advertising agencies are trained to:

1) sell something,

2) sell something, ... and

3) make it pretty so the chairman, while golfing, will receive compliments about his new ad campaign in print or on TV.

Advertising agency copy has to be clever ... it has to be hard-hitting ... let's face it, it has to be *creative*. Unfortunately, that isn't necessarily a formula for effective communications with your customers.

Getting It Right:
Style + Substance = Success!

If the company has survived these several years, and the considerable sum of money that it takes to get to Phase Three, with luck they might make their way to a specialized customer communications agency. Unfortunately, the trauma doesn't end here, it actually begins again.

For example, the approach that we typically recommend is probably perceived as so simple (and radically different from anything they've done in the past), that it only seems to confirm (for the client) the hopelessness of ever "getting it right."

What's the correct approach? It's the antithesis of everything that's been done to date. It's talking *with* customers, not *at* them. It's telling stories, it's nostalgia, it's based on the fundamental premise that people only buy from people they like and trust. It's substance, not sound bites. It's long, even rambling, copy vs. short, staccato headlines. It's reassuring vs. jarring. It's reinforcing vs. breakthrough. It's, well ... "loving."

In fact, the copy approach is so dramatically different from all other types of writing and journalism that the best writers are those with degrees in English or journalism who seem to have high energy and sensitivity ... and who have also been carefully retrained in the specialized precepts of customer communications. Perhaps this can be best illustrated as follows below.

INVERTED PYRAMID

Traditional journalism teaches that you write in an inverted pyramid style. In other words, the most important information comes first, and then gradually the copy peters down to the least important points. The reason for this is that, traditionally, copy editors at newspapers downsize stories with a pair of scissors, clipping up from the bottom in order to make the article fit the available space.

Pyramid-style copy simply doesn't work for customer communications. It's impersonal, jarring and unnatural. It "shouts," but it doesn't "caress." It's not the way we normally communicate as human beings one-to-one with those we trust.

CIRCULAR STYLE

The style of copy needed for effective customer communications is opposite to the pyramid style ... and it is rarely taught in any school of journalism.

It follows the old army maxim of "tell them what you're going to tell them, ... tell them, ... tell them what you told them."

And again, it is the antithesis of traditional journalism.

It's a circular and conversational style of writing.

and then you proceed to summarize your point, bringing the entire "logic-flow" full-circle. It's warm and conversational. It's reassuring.

you then proceed to make your point ....

You start off by telling the customer why you wish them to spend a few moments with you to read this particular material ....

9

What's Different About Customer Communications?

- **Be careful turning your communications over to "professional" journalists and writers who may not understand that "down home" is sometimes better than "big city" talk.**

- **Everything about how you communicate with customers is different. You've got to make their E-string vibrate.**

In 1974 I finished up a two-year appointment as a research associate on the faculty of the Harvard Business School. Leaving academia, I then started, in association with a Boston publisher, a monthly newsletter that went to owners of small businesses to help them learn the techniques taught in any good business school. Things like how to prepare a cash flow statement, how to compute return-on-investment, how to optimize inventory levels, etc. Pretty straightforward stuff.

The newsletter took off like wildfire and became the fastest growing publication of its type in history. Eighteen months later Harcourt, Brace Jovanovich, the then big New York publisher, purchased the property for over $1,000,000.

Let the Professionals Handle It

At the time I strongly suggested to Harcourt that they keep me on to continue writing the material or at least to do the final editing. What I was told, however, is that Harcourt, being such a huge publishing house, had dozens of trained journalists and business writers on its staff. Now that the format of the publication was successfully established, my services were no longer needed.

Again and again I protested and warned them that there was a special technique at work in the editorial approach. A technique that created an almost mystical bond between the publication and the reader. A writing style that was familiar, and admittedly maybe even downright "hokey."

Indeed the writing style reflected my southern Missouri hillbilly roots ... and the down-home authenticity of having worked throughout my youth in a rural community alongside three generations of family who were farmers and entrepreneurs.

Repeatedly, however, I was told, "Take your money, young man and go away. Now is the time to let the professionals handle it."

And They Did

And I did. And they did. And it did. Eighteen months later the publication folded.

So what happened? How could a publication that was the fastest growing of its type in history ... and enjoyed over a 90 percent renewal rate ... go kaput in less than 18 months? Even after a huge, respected publishing house like Harcourt took it over and poured big promotional bucks into it?

That, dear reader, is what this manifesto is all about and, as you're reading through it, hopefully you are learning many of the critical differences between communicating with prospects ... and customers.

Scary Thought...
A Customer Is Like a Spouse

Remember now, we have said that a customer is someone who knows you. You can't fool them. They know your strong points ... and where you stink.

In fact, they are a lot like a spouse. Try as you may, you just can't fool your spouse. They know you even better than you know yourself. Try to weave a little b.s. in front of them and they will toss it in your face.

A customer is like a spouse, an intimate friend, someone you can't fool and shouldn't even try. (But, we try anyway!)

A prospect, in turn, is like a stranger on the street or maybe a slight acquaintance. They may have heard about you through your advertising, they may have some preconceived notions based on what they have heard from friends, but they really do not know you very well.

The Language of Love

And so the way you communicate with customers and prospects is completely different. Linguists and semanticists have shown again and again that the sentence structure, the words that are used (and the words that are left out), the tone, the style, the points of emphasis, the inflection, the "sing-song," everything to do with communication is different depending whether you are speaking with a stranger (prospect) vs. a confidant (customer).

With a stranger there is ritual posturing, a more formal and stilted style, different words, different sentence construction, intonations that can vary from bombastic, as you try to impress the candidate, to deferential as you in turn become impressed.

Pluck the E-String

Joe Sugarman, the famous copywriter and founder of JS&A, a very successful direct marketing and catalog firm, once described it so well. Imagine two guitars on opposite sides of a room. Gently pluck the E-string of one. If both guitars are in perfect tune with each other, the E-string of the other guitar across the room will also vibrate in perfect pitch.

Such it is with customer communications. You and your customers must absolutely resonate ... across a room ... right off the printed page ... through the airwaves into the living room. Otherwise, your effort is wasted.

But, there's more. You not only have to be able to resonate with your customers ... you have to know which string to pluck for each particular audience. With farmers you talk "down home" ... with high fashion retail customers, you may need to mimic *Women's Wear Daily*. Get the editorial "tone" or graphic "timbre" wrong and you'll either sail right over their heads, or hit at their feet with a condescending thud!

Walk the Walk

The bottom line is that you talk to a customer like you talk to a close friend and confidant. You talk in their language and on their level. You don't posture, you don't b.s. them, you don't try to impress them, you don't shade the facts, you certainly don't let the lawyers rework the information into legal conundrums and double speak.

You make sure you're on the right tone and frequency for the audience you're trying to reach ... and then you "walk the walk ... and talk the talk."

John R. Klug

10

What's *Really* Different About Customer Communications?

- **Customer communications is fundamentally different from general advertising and direct mail.**

- **Traditional advertising wants to sell something. Customer communications is concerned only with building and preserving a relationship.**

- **Statement stuffers are an indictment of a company's lack of respect for its customers.**

- **Customer communication should be laser-guided, targeted, personal, local, focused and repetitive.**

A doctor is a doctor. A lawyer is a lawyer. And parts is parts. Right? Dead wrong! Would you hire a cardiac surgeon to do a hip replacement? Would you hire a divorce attorney to draw up the papers for a complicated business acquisition? And more to the point, should you use a general advertising agency to handle customer communications?

Tagging the Bases

Years ago, advertising was advertising. It was all so simple ... you took a look at the "Four Ps" you learned in Marketing 101.

First, you got the **P**roduct defined, next you made sure you had the **P**rice right, then you distributed the product in the right **P**lace. And finally, you took a look at what was the right way to **P**romote the product.

The venerable Madison Avenue agencies did a wonderful job tagging the "P" bases and hitting home runs with homogenous mass advertising throughout the '50s and '60s. Beginning in the early '70s, however, as everything about marketing and advertising became more sophisticated and complex, a new trend began to develop. New *types* of agencies began to hive off the general agencies.

Evolution of
Direct Marketing Agencies

Out of this trend grew the great direct marketing agencies such as Wunderman Ricotta and Klein; Kobs and Brady; Cohn & Wells, and so on. For a while these new types of agencies were shunned, thought to be anomalies and, indeed, the entire direct marketing field was felt to be something of an aberration.

But gradually, both from the client side and from the agency perspective, it was realized that direct marketing was an entirely different and unique advertising skill from that practiced by the general agencies.

Indeed, it almost became axiomatic that, if a general agency would try to do direct response, the effort was doomed to failure, because the disciplines of direct marketing vs. general marketing were so completely different.

Pushers, Pullers, Communicators

And so it is with customer communications. It is unquestionably a new marketing discipline. It is completely, totally, uniquely different from direct marketing and/or general marketing. And indeed, almost invariably, when anyone not completely specialized in customer communications attempts such an effort, it's doomed to failure.

Let's see if we can explain some of the differences.

For ease, we're going to combine the marketing practiced by general agencies ("Pullers") and that created by direct marketing agencies ("Pushers") into what we'll call *"Traditional Marketing."* And, we're going to call the craft of *"Customer Communications"* just that.

Traditional push and pull marketing is concerned only with selling something. Customer communications is concerned only with building and preserving a relationship.

How You Say It

This subtle but critical distinction pervades every aspect of customer marketing. As we've discussed, the "copy voice" in customer communications is completely different from the "in your face" approach often taken in traditional marketing.

Where You Say It

And, again, the types of media are totally different. For example, traditional marketing would use radio, television, direct mail … whereas customer communications would use a rich mix of personal interactive media such as personal letters, newsletters, telephone follow-up, inbound 800 numbers, and so on.

So, the tone of voice must be different. And the media you use to speak with your customer is different.

What You Say

And, the things you talk to your customer *about* are completely different. For example, much of traditional marketing is like dropping cluster bombs from B-52s. It's an indiscriminate saturation technique, and your only hope is that your message falls close enough to someone "out there" to have an impact.

Customer communications is the antithesis. It's laser-guided, targeted, personal (notice we didn't say computerized), local, focused, interactive and repetitive (can we ever say "I love you" too many times?).

Nostalgia, Ethics, Satisfaction

Let's review again just how different successful customer communications is from other types of advertising and promotion:

- **General advertising** is the world of clever jingles and fast action video.
- **Direct mail** is the world of response drivers, "Johnson boxes" and benefit headlines.
- In turn, some of the most successful **customer communications** we've ever seen (as measured in ROI, and sales increases) involved no sales copy at all.

For example, we've spent years assisting one of the largest retailers in the country communicate with their premier customer group. In this case, we talk in a nostalgic sense about the history of the firm, what the company stands for, community events, how to get satisfaction if you, as a customer, ever have a problem, etc.

Pretty boring stuff. And we dwell on it again and again and again. Year after year. With trackable sales results well beyond expectations.

Nostalgia, ethics, satisfaction. Those are but a few of the ingredients of a credible and a successful dialog with your most important asset. Your customers.

Corporate Cynicism

Having considered what works best when you communicate with your customers, let's consider what you shouldn't do. For example, the corporate cynicism of some companies toward their customers seems to know no bounds.

So little is their regard for the intelligence and integrity of customers that certain credit card companies, retailers, public utilities, etc., will routinely offer virtually any product or service in the billing statement if it might make a few extra dollars for the company.

You've all seen the flyers and mini-brochures in the billing statements for everything from belt buckles to vacuum cleaners. For the most part, these so-called "statement stuffers" are a testament to, and an indictment of, the lack of respect and regard for the intelligence of the most valuable asset the company has ... its customers.

In the Long Run, You'll Die

Rather than take the opportunity to communicate positive and useful messages to their customers, companies are slowly destroying the franchise that they have created with their customers by the mindless and short-term use of third-party promotional pieces. Statement stuffers are like cocaine. They make your P&L feel wonderful in the short run. They're addictive. But in the long run, you'll die.

Stated differently, if you can't figure out something appropriate to say to your customer in a billing statement, then don't say anything at all. For God's sake, don't put in a mindless, impersonal, third-party buckslip for belt buckles or encyclopedias.

Respect Customers

Never forget Rule #1 of customer communications ... customers know you better than you know yourself .... they're smart ... and they can make (or break) you faster than anyone.

Coca-Cola learned this lesson real fast when they fiddled with the original Coke formula. And G.M. could have been saved a lot of embarrassment (and expense) if only they had more carefully exposed the Caprice Classic design to more customer focus groups — ahead of time.

Respect customers!

11

Here's Where We've Been

We've covered a lot of ground in just a few short pages. Basically, here's a summary:

- In the 1980s, with everyone's boat rising in the water, Madison Avenue had a field day. Brands were strong, disposable income was rising and marketing was like shooting fish in a barrel.
- Things have leveled off in the '90s. Bills have come due, national income is level and declining and even the lowest interest rates in a generation are having little visible effect on the economy. The name of the game has shifted to holding on to what you've got, providing value, retaining your present customers and building long-term relationships.
- Customers are different from prospects. On the surface, it would seem obvious, and to point out this fact could be trite. However, virtually all advertising, promotion and communications is approached as if a customer were identical to a prospect. It simply won't work. Customer communication is truly a unique new marketing discipline.

- Customers must be addressed in a totally different tone of voice from prospects. You must speak the "language of love." Your customers absolutely cannot be fooled. You share an intimacy with them and must speak to them in a familiar language of shared experience. You've got to "walk the walk ... and talk the talk."

- Not only must the language to customers be unique, but the media must be carefully selected as well. Customers desire interaction. They want to "mix" with their media. They want to be approached on many levels and through many media. Not only must the message and the tone of voice be right, but the media must be appropriate as well. Many of the media available and appropriate today to reach and interact with customers have never been considered by marketers.

- Video game designers and Hollywood filmmakers truly know more about communications in the 1990s than most marketing executives. That's why the creative epicenter of the world has shifted toward Hollywood.

- Not only are traditional agencies ill-suited to reach customers ... even traditional journalism teaches inappropriate techniques. It can take years to break the "pyramidal" writing style as taught in journalism schools ... and convert to the simple-to-conceive, but difficult-to-execute, circular style of *"tell 'em what you're going to tell 'em; tell 'em; tell 'em what you told 'em."*

- Customer communications is a superior investment. You'll get far more sales per dollar spent than with any other marketing strategy. And, your per unit marketing expenditures will decline.

- We predict that marketing priorities in the 1990s will "invert" with the major emphasis shifting from new prospect advertising ... to maintaining and building sales from existing customers.

12

Here's How You Get Started

If you find the concepts we've discussed to be of interest, and want to take the next step, you should first conduct a "Communications Audit." This audit will address your present communications efforts and propose future customer communications programs that you may wish to consider. To help you get started, attached is the summary of an audit we did for a disguised client, "ABC Bank." We hope it's helpful.

In closing ... *You* are the one who has to decide if you believe that customers are your major asset ... whether customer marketing truly is a unique new marketing discipline ... and whether customer communications offers an untapped opportunity for your company. If so, it would be a privilege to discuss this fascinating field with you.

Thank you for your interest.

CCG

Customer Communications Group, Inc.
12600 W. Cedar Drive
Denver, CO 80228
303-986-3000

Appendix

ABC Bank INTEGRATED COMMUNICATIONS PROGRAM

Priority	Customer/Prospect Category	Recommended Tool	Frequency	Measurement
1	High Value Deposit (Includes Alternative Investments) (Top 20 Percent of Deposits)	Personalized Letter from Branch Manager, with Customized Incentives	Monthly	• Acquisition Cost per Account • Total Relationship Value • Net Retention
2	High Value Real Estate Loan Customers (Single Service Jumbo Mortgage)	Targeted Pre-approved Credit Card/Home Equity Mailings	Quarterly	• Acquisition Cost per Account • Total Relationship Value
3	Other Deposit Customers	Statements or Mailed Newsletter (for CD Customers)	Quarterly	• Net Retention • Telephone Readership Surveys (Annual) • Response Rate
4	Other Loan Customers	50% Bank/Product, 50% Information, With Response Device (High Value Customers Included in the Mailings)		
5	Deposit Non-Customers	Retail Advertising	Five 8-Week Campaigns	• Deposit Retention Rate • Acquisition Cost per Account
6	Real Estate Loan Non-Customers	Loan Officer to Realtor Communications Program, Mailed to 100% of Realtors in Loan Officer Territories	Quarterly	• Response Rates from Mailings • Calls Generated • Loan Volume (Over Time)

Principals of CCG

John R. Klug
Chairman and Chief Executive Officer

John R. Klug is Chairman and Chief Executive Officer of Customer Communications Group, Inc. He founded the company in 1977.

Prior to founding CCG, Mr. Klug served as an officer in the U.S. Army stationed at the Pentagon. He was also a research associate and faculty member at the Harvard Business School, from which he received a Master's in Business Administration in 1972. Mr. Klug has 25 years of experience in publishing, direct marketing, telemarketing, newsletter editorial and production.

Also a nationally renowned business consultant, Mr. Klug has worked with such companies as General Motors, Federal Express, Victoria Station, Sea Pines Resorts and Hunt Oil.

Thad D. Peterson
President and General Manager

Thad D. Peterson is President and General Manager of CCG. Mr. Peterson has 12 years of retail bank marketing experience and has held Vice President, Senior Vice President and Executive Vice President retail marketing positions, most recently as Director of Marketing for Glendale Federal Bank.

Mr. Peterson has six years of advertising experience with Ketchum Communications and other San Francisco based agencies. His former employers include BankAmerica Cheque Corporation, Bank of America, EurekaBank, Glendale Federal Bank, and Allen Dorward Advertising.

He has written several articles and is a frequent speaker on the subject of customer communications and database marketing. Mr. Peterson received a B.S. in Education from the University of Idaho.